FAITH in MOTION

FAITH in MOTION

A COMPILATION OF POEMS
FROM THE THRONE ROOM
OF HEAVEN

ZION JOHNSON

Faith in Motion © Copyright 2022 Zion Johnson

All rights reserved. No part of this publication may be reproduced, distributed or transmitted in any form or by any means, including photocopying, recording, or other electronic or mechanical methods, without the prior written permission of the publisher, except in the case of brief quotations embodied in critical reviews and certain other noncommercial uses permitted by copyright law.

Although the author and publisher have made every effort to ensure that the information in this book was correct at press time, the author and publisher do not assume and hereby disclaim any liability to any party for any loss, damage, or disruption caused by errors or omissions, whether such errors or omissions result from negligence, accident, or any other cause.

Adherence to all applicable laws and regulations, including international, federal, state and local governing professional licensing, business practices, advertising, and all other aspects of doing business in the US, Canada or any other jurisdiction is the sole responsibility of the reader and consumer.

Neither the author nor the publisher assumes any responsibility or liability whatsoever on behalf of the consumer or reader of this material. Any perceived slight of any individual or organization is purely unintentional.

The resources in this book are provided for informational purposes only and should not be used to replace the specialized training and professional judgment of a health care or mental health care professional.

Neither the author nor the publisher can be held responsible for the use of the information provided within this book. Please always consult a trained professional before making any decision regarding treatment of yourself or others.

ISBN (paperback): 979-8-88759-342-5
ISBN (eBook): 979-8-88759-343-2

Hebrews 11:1 NKJV

Now faith is the substance of things hoped for, the evidence of things not seen.

Scan the QR Code for exclusive content by joining the Faith In Motion E-Mail list!

TABLE OF CONTENTS

9 FOREWORD
Janelle Johnson

11 INTRODUCTION

15 CHAPTER ONE

35 CHAPTER TWO

47 CHAPTER THREE

59 CHAPTER FOUR

73 CHAPTER FIVE

85 CHAPTER SIX

97 CHAPTER SEVEN

FOREWORD

Often times, we do not see our creativity. Knowing that we have our own uniqueness of creativity that only our Abba Father can superimpose in our spirit is beyond our understanding.

This book is a form of worship. Allow your spirit to guide you through peace and get you on course for a life of joy.

As you read this art of hope, I pray your destinies align, you prophesy your today and be catapulted into your tomorrow.

Receive an implantation of new oil, new freedom, and prosperity in your hands. While reading, you will feel the power of Holy Spirit. Embrace It! Embrace the anointing and apply these simple tools to move forward in your Kingdom assignments.

Don't waver, move forward!

Regardless of where you are in Faith; Receive! Embrace! Live how Abba Father predestined you to live!

Psalm 51:10 NIV

Create in me a pure heart, O God, and renew a steadfast spirit within me.

Janelle Johnson

INTRODUCTION

On December 20th, 2020 something happened. At Hub Vineland (in Vineland, New Jersey), a mantle was dropped from Heaven. This mantle was by no means ordinary. The only word fit to describe it would be… supernatural! Extraordinary is how it should be described. Writing this book has been in my spirit heavily. Now I'm taking the step and operating in faith to get this out to the masses.

This work of art has been brewing in my belly for a while now. It took a while for my flesh to catch what Holy Spirit has been speaking to me. Holy Spirit (The Helper) helped me figure out exactly what He has been speaking to me. God has a way of letting His children know exactly which way to go.

I've always had a passion for writing poetry. This passion dates back all the way to my days in elementary school. Up until 2020, I didn't realize how I can use one of the gifts that God gave me to glorify Him. It wasn't until I got passionate about Him that all of this clicked! It's like a key got put into an ignition and I really started getting somewhere. The fire that was sparked on the inside started to flow out!

There is not one poem that you read or feel throughout this work of art where I took the lead. Holy Spirit is the Captain and Chief, Zion took a seat. He gave this through me so it would connect to whomever is in need. Young, old, or anywhere in between this will surely be a thrill to read. Not in the sense of drama or suspense, but in a way that is relatable. At times it will be intense but know it's all in steps, even diamonds before they become diamonds are pressed.

The relationship we have with Holy Spirit is the most important relationship we should and can have while on this Earth! Abba the Father is on His throne, Yeshua the Son is at His right hand seated in Heavenly places;

Ephesians 2:6 NKJV

"and raised us up together, and made us sit together in the heavenly places in Christ Jesus,";

Holy Spirit is down here on Earth filling up all of the empty spaces!

I PRAY THAT FROM THIS BOOK YOU GET EXACTLY WHAT HOLY SPIRIT HAS INTENDED FOR YOU TO RECEIVE! THIS WAS WRITTEN JUST FOR YOU!

ENJOY!

December 21st, 2020 12:04 am

Obedience

Better than sacrifice.

Obedience is key.

As a child of God, it is what you need.

A derivative of the word hupakoé in Greek.

It basically means submission to the One who speaks.

Abba is sitting on His seat; this Earth is a stool for His feet.

We are the pillars that hold up His Kingdom, we stand in between.

Luke 3:22 sets the scene; the Father's only begotten Seed listened to what was spoken to Him in eternity.

We met God before we just don't remember, that's why Holy Spirit is here, He is the Messenger.

The only way we can hear from the Lord in all of His splendor is if we surrender.

No, obedience isn't weak!

It actually shows our position lined up with the King.

We all can't just do as we please, that doesn't benefit the rest of the team.

Whether it's now or later every creature will have to take a knee.

I'd rather do it now while the option remains free.

Through my obedience, I know a spot in the Kingdom is reserved for me!

December 22nd, 2020 1:23 am

Discipline

A disciple is disciplined.

Holy Spirit lives within, He is the One to help reveal to us what it takes to be disciplined.

The Kingdom of Heaven has an army, militant.

A soldier can't fight in a battle if there is no discipline.

If you go rogue, you're out on your own road.

Abba built a shelter for us, but we can't dwell in it if we're out for our own goals.

The word discipline literally means the practice of training people to obey.

Get that through your brain!

Don't worry, I'm not just writing to you this is for me as well, don't forget my pen is the one that hit this page.

The code of behavior is passed down from the Savior.

He basically said, "Follow Me while I'm here and your eternal life will be here later."

Lack of discipline will get you caught up burning in the pit of that lake filled with fire like a piece of gasoline drenched paper!

Discipline yourself now, so you can bear witness to the King and display your glory with Him before your Maker!

December 23rd, 2020 10:56 pm

Enlistment

A little more than 2,000 years ago Jesus took a faith-filled walk to Calvary.

Coincidentally we also partake in a faith-filled walk into the Heavenly Calvary.

Our yes isn't a mere yes we say to impress.

It's a declaration we make not just to get out of our mess, but with that YES, we now get put to the test.

Just like a natural army, that yes comes with pressure to impress the One who sits above that is better than the rest!

What's your rank?

Where's your sword?

Can't bring a gun to a sword fight, of this I am sure.

The enemy is creeping around seeking whom he may devour, I'm on the side of the Lord so the victory is ours!

Keep your armor on at all times!

Get ready for some long nights, Light penetrates through darkness He's brighter than all sights!

This isn't for the weak trust and believe, you're gonna have to fight for flight to be seen.

Earthly battles must take place to earn your stripes.

Even the Earth and all its vastness wasn't formed in one night.

Yeshua died for your life!

Think about that every time you decide to do something impure in His sight.

Saving souls and catching demon bodies must be more than a hobby.

The gulag won't last forever, now is the time to take part in the lobby.

December 25th, 2020 12:16 pm

Focus

This is something I've been lacking lately.

Have been seeking heavily, and it's something I'm slowly grasping.

Trying to stay on this narrow road but stumbling blocks keep on slowing down my traction.

The sad part is distractions are happening because of my actions.

See one thing and I'm barely thinking before reacting.

Then POOF!

It blows up in my face.

In tears some nights and days in front of the Lord on my face.

Thinking "Why am I this way?"

I try my best daily.

But... do I?

Am I always putting my best foot forward or am I doing what I can just to scoot by?

Abba, I know You know my heart, it was wicked.

I focused on Your Son, and He fixed it!

But I'll admit it, there's times where I catch myself slipping.

You chastise me to correct me because sin is what You don't want me to live in.

Can't take my eyes off You, that's how I walk on water.

Gotta stop focusing on me and start to FOCUS on You, my Heavenly Father!

December 26th, 2020 11:45pm

Exposure

There's something about Light.

It makes darkness flee; in a dark room it's tough to see.

Ask Saul when those scales were on, it was hard to perceive, but when they got ripped off, he was set free.

True indeed, the Truth shall set me free!

A lot of individuals are walking around blind because of their fear to speak.

I must etch exactly what was given to me, we can't eat fruit off of every tree.

Intermingling with sin leaves you with STD's.

Sexually Transmitted Demons that's adultery!

One of the most important, no the MOST important commandment my LORD gave me, is to have no other idols take His seat!

Sadly, believers want to conform to this world and not be transformed by the renewing of the mind.

The masses and the media have most hypnotized.

Remember, we're Christians parenthesis Followers of Christ; mass doesn't start at nine.

These pagan practices must get left behind!

How long will it take the ones on the fence to decide?

Guess what, the enemy is great at camouflage.

That fence is where he resides.

December 27th, 2020 9:10 pm

Persecution

Persecution is coming, that hour is near.

If you look around the world it's already here.

Jesus got persecuted; as His followers it is our portion.

When you face trials and go through tribulations remember Who is important.

When you hit those blocks on the road to the Kingdom know the enemy formed them.

No weapon formed against you shall prosper… NOT EVEN ONE!

If your faith is firm in God's Son, know that you already won!

Sheep prepared for the slaughter is what we are.

If you dwell in the shelter of Adonai, He is never far.

If you take a glimpse of what is happening overseas, you'll see blood being shed of those who are on the winning team.

That could easily be you or me.

Satan hates to see the Kingdom proceed.

Succeed is what we will do, the gospel of Christ is tried and true!

No matter what they try to do, ALWAYS REMAIN YOU!

Keep your shield up to block the arrows, remember God hardened the heart of Pharoah.

The path to the gates of Heaven is narrow.

Sacrifice comes with a cost, and so does this walk.

Will you lay down your life for the One who gave His life up for you?

December 27th, 2020 11:15 pm

Shalom

Peace that surpasses all understanding.

That comes when Abba's shelter is what you reside under.

When your faith comes without wonder you know where you're standing.

The Prince of Peace delights in me!

The Lord of lords what a sight to see.

He does not give me a spirit of fear.

I must cast all my cares on Him because He cares for me.

That's real deep, but deeper is the love He feels for me.

I command and decree peace for me!

Exclaim that over yourself: PEACE FOR ME!

That whole portion is for you, not just a piece.

The breath of God is in your lungs, so stop, and breathe.

Tranquility sounds like a lot for me, but Jesus brings that every time He knocks on your heart and pleads.

Yes, He intercedes to ensure that we have what we need.

Can you take a second to imagine Christ yelling "Father Please!"?

What's intriguing is Jesus couldn't spell eternal peace without the word WE!

Think about it, Jesus died for you so you could share in His eternal peace.

December 28th, 2020 12:02 am

Ground-Crew

On this Earth we are the hands and feet of the Lord.

Of this I am sure, a workman approved is what we all aim to be.

One that can handle the Word of Truth no matter how hot it gets.

Nebuchadnezzar can't turn the furnace up to a high enough degree!

I'm about my Father's business; all for His glory.

This is non-fiction, this is not a story.

A mouthpiece for Him is what I must be, after all I'm made in His image.

This side of eternity is preparation for the big leagues, this is merely a scrimmage.

Popeye got stronger when he ate spinach, I grow stronger when I'm in line with Yahweh's vision.

We are sent here on a mission to carry out His plan and do His bidding.

He is sitting on the throne yes, I said sitting!

The weight is not hard to bear because Jesus did all the heavy lifting.

The task is at hand, the way to accomplish it is God filled living.

We have been commissioned to heal the sick, cast out devils, speak in new tongues, and most importantly to spread and preach His gospel to the ends of the Earth.

In order to ascend into Heaven, I must do the work of my Father on the ground first.

December 30th, 2020 12:52 am

Action!

Abba is up there on His throne watching it all unfold.

His throne is literally the Director's Chair.

We are actors in a way because we act like we're from here.

It started making sense since I stopped and stared at myself in the mirror.

We are from eternity, eternally we won't live here.

When we sin against the Father, we grieve Holy Spirit.

He says, "You're hurting Me!"

The Great Physician is the only One in that position to add or subtract to this life that we were given.

But the catch is, we have the choice of how we live it.

When He says "Cut!", and plays it back will your purity be intact?

The Body has been attacked, but our minds should never lack!

Time to throw away the baby food; no longer can we afford to be nourished with similac.

There's no redo's this footage is concrete, it's the prequel to the sequel and I must do what is asked and expected of me like Ezekiel.

It's time to show the world what following Christ truly means!

My God is the Great Elohim!

Our yoke is solid, no scheme from the enemy shall come in between.

Gotta get like Daniel down on your knees, but not for everyone to see.

Intimacy should be kept between Abba and me.

Let the Lord write out the script and you just read instead of allowing carnality to intervene.

Let Christ do what He does and intercede.

Holy Spirit already knows the ropes, allow Him to take the lead!

December 30th, 2020 1:09 am

Recognition

If we don't recognize the Lord when He speaks our fruit is of the wrong tree.

You can't mistake an apple for an orange, or even oatmeal for porridge.

We often try to seek for similarities but there is no Kingdom thesaurus.

What we need is discernment!

That will give us the ability to discern when the Lord is downloading within us a word man.

Man there is used in reference as mankind.

At times we confuse the Word of the Lord with the Adversary's land lies.

We have these feeble man minds that find it hard to even know our pants size.

Stop trying to put on clothes you pick out for yourself!

Allow Him to clothe you with the garments He prepared for you.

That spirit of doubt and unbelief must go!

If it remains, you'll never know even if Abba told you so.

It's tough at times I know, but when you're in His frequency it comes naturally, it just flows.

This is based on relationship.

You'll know His voice and you'll know His touch from the crown of your head down to the bottom of your soles.

If you don't know ask Holy Spirit, trust and believe He will let you know!

When you're under the shelter of the Most High there is nowhere else you'll want to go.

Man's words have nothing on His presence; trust me when you feel Him, you'll know!

December 30th, 2020 11:34 pm

Holy

The angels walk around His throne and praise Him, they have been for eternity.

They shout, "Holy, Holy, Holy is the LORD God Almighty!"

We are made in His image, so in turn we are created and called to be holy.

Adonai said it Himself, it is written: "Be holy, for I am holy."

Holiness is achievable, but it must happen in the mind first.

In order to obtain it we must understand how His mind works.

Consecration must be made for Abba every day.

We must live out His Word and exemplify Him in action and in speech.

We should not be exalted but the One within us must be lifted up!

Set-apart for His glory isn't just a cute motto.

Hallowed isn't just a word in prayer, in honoring Him it's the first step on the stairs.

Always prepare to be prepared.

Holy is a four-letter word: it's a noun, adjective, and verb.

Isn't it something that there is a Heavenly Deity waiting outside of this universe for you and me?

Relationship is what He seeks, don't allow anything to intervene and clog your ears so you can't hear when He speaks.

His will is perfect, and His love is insane.

Holy, Holy, Holy, Alleluia!

All praise be to our Holy King!

January 1st, 2021 11:42 pm

Beginning

The new Gregorian year has just begun.

God's work isn't just starting technically speaking He already won!

5781 is the year that He is at the door.

It's time to wake up and receive His pour.

New year, new revelation, deeper relationship.

Can't do like last year and play the fence or take offense.

Jesus is Lord of all, He is the reason for our salvation.

John 1:1 says He is the beginning!

Apply the Word daily to your life.

The living Word is Christ let Him change you from the inside.

Might have to break off from some people and refrain from unedifying activities.

Lift weights supernaturally, train your spirit.

The new year is here so it's time to be fearless!

Shake yourself off and allow Abba to shape you up.

Let Him trim off the split ends if you do it alone you might end up cut.

Trust me, throughout the process you'll look rough, but do what you can and through it all have faith.

God doesn't make mistakes and when it comes to His kids, He don't play!

Begin to ask and seek exactly what He has for you.

He brought you through last year so you can see this one all the way through.

January 2nd, 2021 10:51 pm

Hunger

Hunger.

It's that feeling you feel in your belly when you know it's time to eat.

Physically you need it to stay alive so on the contrary, spiritually you need to eat, or you'll die.

Sure, a five for five will temporarily satisfy… but it's not sustaining.

Fast food just isn't the same as a homemade meal.

Nothing like sitting at the table and hearing about your loved one's day.

It's dinner time every time we read the Word.

The Lord provides a gourmet buffet!

Don't eat too fast you'll get full quick and there's a chance you'll regurgitate.

You must digest and chew slowly; have patience!

It's not going anywhere.

Take a couple bites and wash it down with some prayer.

Once you have your plate pace yourself.

There's a lot more where that came from.

Our spiritual food is from the same place we came from; the mind of The Great One who is ancient!

Stop being famished, understand this;

The knowledge of this world does damage.

Read the Word and worship that's your fork and your spoon.

He already has your plate ready, just pull up a chair.

The Father will give you your fill of breakfast, lunch, and dinner.

His food described in 3 words:

Organic, Sustaining, Unchanging.

Tevet 20, 5781 10:56 pm

Fear

Fear is the faith of the devil.

If you fall into it, he begins to pull the strings like Geppetto.

You cannot serve two masters!

You either love one or hate the other.

Is fear your master or in Christ are you an overcomer?

When it comes down to cover the question is, who are you under?

Does fear have you gripped, or do you have that wicked spirit's number?

Often, I wonder as believers if we comprehend the power in our tongue.

I know I'm just a man, but I belong to the One who said it is finished and, when He walks in evil can't stand!

EVERYTHING kneels before the King!

That means fear takes a knee.

Wait a minute, if fear is submissive to Him by association doesn't that mean fear is submissive to me?

Greater is He that is in me than he that is in this world.

That second he is lower cased just like the ruler of this age.

The enemy will have his day, but today I decree fear will flee in Jesus name!

Make this declaration before you turn this page, read these next lines aloud and proclaim.

FEAR HAS NO HOLD OVER ME!

I AM FREE TODAY!

JESUS LIVES IN ME AND HE IS HERE TO STAY!

Tevet 21 5781 10:45 pm

New Shoes

They just have that fresh smell to them.

The soles are untouched, and the laces are woven but you must lace them up.

A perfect fit is far and few to come between.

John the Baptist wasn't even feeling worthy enough to touch the Messiah's feet.

We are holy ground walking!

We are what Moses had to remove his shoes for.

Stomping on the enemy is what these kicks are used for!

New paths come with new destinations.

The wilderness is a path on the road less traveled you must chase it.

Without the proper shoes your soul is exposed.

Isn't that something, a sole is what comforts the bottom of your toes.

The gospel is what we must walk in, literally walk it out not just talk it!

Faith is what we must leap with!

Tell me, how can we jump if we allow ourselves to get stumped every time we step in puddles and get our feet wet?

Witchcraft operating in the church, religious folks scared to get their feet swept.

Take a deep breath.

One step at a time is all it takes.

The children of Israel didn't cross over in one day, it took movement, endurance, and a set pace.

Their shoes lasted them the whole way.

Yes, they had delays, but they made mistakes then so we don't walk in those shoes today.

Use your brain!

Next time you put on your shoes truly think about what you're doing.

We're ambassadors for the Kingdom.

Wherever we step the King is moving!

New shoes = New direction

Tevet 22 5781 11:13 pm

Invitation

Access is given with invitation.

Invitation to His holy presence must be taken when it is received.

To truly comprehend and understand the things that are unseen, we need to sit at His feet.

The aroma of His fragrance is so sweet, leaving it leaves us incomplete.

When that invitation gets received there's no such thing as in too deep.

Holy Spirit groans for us while Jesus intercedes.

That invitation was sent when His blood was shed!

But when it lands in our hands what we do is up to us.

It would be foolish to return that message back to the Sender unopened.

Often, that invitation gets no focus and goes unnoticed; only until we feel hopeless, do we ever take the time to notice.

Clarity is key.

Can't get distracted just because we know the Door is open.

Regain your focus!

If you receive, please receive wholeheartedly, don't do it halfway.

Don't let the opportunity burn out like ash in an ashtray.

Yeshua is the Pathway!

He invited you in so go in that way!

Everyone doesn't get that chance to get called and sit with the Father.

When you are summoned consider that as an honor.

Tevet 26 5781 9:58 am

Royal Blood Was Shed

Blood is what keeps us alive.

It pumps through all our veins; without it we can't survive.

I got a question.

How many times will you die?

Once or twice?

Are you existing or are you alive?

Where will you inhabit for eternity?

Are you a part of the Royal Bloodline?

Sorry, I said I had a question, but I rattled off like 5.

Just take a second or two to think about it.

What did you realize?

We might come from different parents biologically, but if you're a child of Abba we have the same blood.

I'm not talking about O-Negative or O-Positive; I'm speaking on the Blood that washed away your sins!

It's comfortable to walk in like you slipped on a pair of moccasins.

That Blood was shed on a cross, it dripped onto the ground, and Jesus came off!

Didn't God create mankind from the dust of the ground?

From dust we came and back to dust we will return.

When He returns, He's coming back for His bride.

In order to get that transfusion, you need to become born again first!

Tevet 29 5781 11:32 pm

Paid In Full

How much did you cost?

That's a real question, I'm writing directly to you.

You were expensive, every ounce of His blood was payment for you.

The Earthly things that are precious is what money can't buy.

Money can't buy love and true love doesn't lie.

You see love starts in the mind.

It's the purest feeling.

Jesus loves you so much, there's no purer feeling.

His body was beaten, battered, and bruised.

He did that for you!

Went through all that suffering and torture for you.

Movies can't capture everything He endured.

If you watched Him get whipped your jaw would've been on the floor.

Trust and believe it was worse than what we see on a screen.

Our Savior was disfigured beyond recognition and hung on a tree.

That was a pivotal day for you on Calvary!

It changed history!

Your debt was paid in full!

He gave His life up and laid it down for you.

Think about it for a while, He put His life on the line, truly take some time.

Think about the sacrifice that offers you eternal life, let that sit in your mind.

Your life was paid for, it was purchased with His Blood!

He doesn't want Heaven without you, never think you're not enough!

Tevet 30 5781 11:52 pm

Chow Time

There's never a better time than now to eat.

Chew, digest, then speak.

As human beings we love to tell others about what we just tasted.

For the palate to become mature, there must be patience.

There's an arrangement that our taste buds have with our brain.

With the tongue we taste.

Our brain either says yay or nay.

If it tastes great, we want to run and tell everyone.

If we eat too quick, we throw up.

Instead of getting nourished it comes right back up.

Waste is supposed to come out of our other spout but sometimes it flows from the mouth.

Did you take time to eat and then speak?

If you haven't, listen closer to what you read.

The spirit feeds when the flesh is asleep.

It's tough to eat when you haven't developed your spiritual teeth.

Shevat 2 5781 11:41 pm

His Grace

Father Your grace is so sweet!

You saved a sinner like me.

I once was lost, but You found me.

Was blind but now I can see.

Before You allowed me to see my physical body, You knew me.

Every tendon and tissue, You knew the end result before You began.

Your thoughts outnumber the sands of this Earth.

The crazy part is, I am one of those thoughts.

You know me better than I know myself!

Grace and Your love go hand in hand.

I'm glad I'm under the protection of Your right one.

Never felt like the right one until I was touched by the Right One!

Now that old life is done and in Christ new life comes!

You created me then but when I accepted Your Son Jesus, I was made new!

My body is a temple for You!

My life is not my own.

To You I belong.

I give myself to You as freely as You give Your grace.

That's mind, heart, body, soul, and spirit.

You are always with me.

It's comforting to lean on You especially after a hard day.

In order to serve and love You fully, You must be given access to occupy my heart's space.

Shevat 3 5781 11:50 pm

Presence

His presence is the ultimate present!

When dwelling at His feet nothing but obedience is accepted.

A tangible feeling that our flesh can't obtain.

Our spirit on the other hand desires that connection to Abba is maintained.

Nothing else will do!

Our destiny abides in His arms.

Run to Him and stick to His words like glue.

If only we had a clue of what it's truly like to sit with You.

It's something that can't be taken for granted.

My God, Jehovah made this universe, He is outside of time.

Yeshua the Son is always in His midst and as believers in us His Spirit resides.

Children of the Most High yearn for His presence.

There's nothing better than being with the Father!

Sitting with Him is so sweet; I never want to leave!

That Heavenly visitation is the other end of the best invitation.

We can't take for granted the information instilled in those situations.

Lips quiver and voices change intonation when the Maker of all creation makes Himself seen.

Get to your secret place and dwell in His presence.

Let Him unfold those layers of baggage from the seams.

Shevat 4 5781 11:41 pm

Workman Approved

On this Earth we are the hands and feet of the Lord.

Of this I am sure, a workman approved is what we all aim to be.

One that can handle the Word of Truth no matter how hot it gets.

Nebuchadnezzar can't turn the furnace up to a high enough degree.

I got Holy Spirit's fire burning inside of me!

No water can put out nor quench this flame.

Since I became born again nothing has been the same!

I may have hit a couple of blocks that caused me to stumble but, that's a part of the growing process I can see the stubble.

My foundation is built on the Corner Stone, the enemy can keep the rubble.

Daily I fight spiritually, carnality is the struggle.

When it doesn't seem so great, I remember those three Hebrew boys.

Bowing down to that wretched idol was not an option nor was it a choice.

They were focused on the Lord's voice.

His Word keeps me solid, quick on my feet, and poised.

Poison is what the enemy intends to do to our minds, he intends to pollute it.

When in warfare remember, we are connected to the Holy Vine.

The weapons of our warfare are not carnal; they have the power to loose and bind!

January 21st, 2021 12:59 am

Repentance

"Repent for the Kingdom of Heaven is near."

My Lord's sentiment is clear.

Without repentance one cannot inherit the Kingdom and enjoy all of His glory.

Asking for forgiveness and going back to sin is sloppy grace!

Every time we habitually sin, we spit right in Jesus' face and nail Him back onto the cross when being next to the Father is His rightful place.

God knows we are not perfect.

We're human, our nature is fallen so we are destined to make mistakes.

But never did the Lord of hosts ask us to lie to His face.

Repentance truthfully is turning away from your sin and coming into covenant with Abba to never do it again.

Ever ask yourself; "Why do I remain in the same cycles?"

Instead of making 180 degree turns you just continue to spin.

Let that sink in.

He loves our repentance because He hates our sin.

Lack of direction always requires correction.

You must know why you are walking down the path you are traveling on.

True repentance is partnered with submission, it's a tried and true method.

Lack of honesty with yourself will never let it take place.

"Repent for the Kingdom of Heaven is at hand."

Repentance is needed in order to walk through those gates.

REPENT!

Shevat 9 5781 12:20 am

Ananias

Where is the modern-day Ananias?

Without Ananias, Paul would've stayed Saul and remained silent.

The scales would've remained over his eyes.

Masses of people would've remained blind.

We might not have received revelation the way we received it in the Word.

Think about it.

If Ananias stayed afraid two thirds of the New Testament we have today would've never occurred.

Disobeying Yeshua Hamashiach is absurd!

Sadly, most do it daily I concur.

Sinning goes from thoughts to actions, nouns to verbs.

When is the last time you were told to rip scales off someone's eyes?

Were you afraid of the warfare so you left the assignment behind?

Most of what we do is not for us, it's for the person that person will touch!

I could only imagine being in Ananias' shoes, that road to Saul must've been tough.

He had to be thinking about all that Saul had done to his brothers and sisters which was corrupt.

Sure enough, he took that hike.

Jesus told him to do so.

Think about that the next time you get called to go to a place that no one goes.

Shevat 16 5781 11:42 pm

Operation

The only way you can discern what spirit is in operation, is if you're taking heed to what Holy Spirit is saying.

Listen.

Observe.

He speaks to us in many ways, more than just words.

For we battle NOT against flesh and blood!

The weapons of our warfare are NOT carnal!

Do you recognize fear and anger manifesting within that man on the bar stool?

Go wherever He tells you to go!

Every soul deserves to hear the Truth.

The gospel of Christ isn't reserved for believers!

We are called to be followers of our Leader.

It's for the Gentiles too, can't afford to misconstrue the vision like Peter.

These disembodied beings are full of intelligence that surpasses human comprehension.

Extraction must occur for you to step in what Abba created you to step in.

Do you get it?

Faith is what pleases Him, that's our greatest weapon!

It's hard to stop a habit once it starts, but when you're covered by the Blood you must be consecrated unto Him, set apart.

The Word of God reveals the true intent of the heart.

When you operate within Him you follow after His heart.

If you don't believe me just read about Noah and the ark.

January 30th, 2021 10:59 pm

On Earth As In Heaven

This is not just a part of a prayer.

We are mandated, commissioned to make the Kingdom appear.

Let me be clear, the King reigns!

He is sitting on His throne.

It's my job to make this Earth look like His home!

Wickedness prevails when we fail to remove the veil.

Glory fell when Jesus came back from conquering Hell!

We expel any scheme that the enemy tries to sell.

The firmament is a dome but it's really a big mirror.

We should reflect the Father, with Him our vision is made clearer.

We are His workmanship approved to do good works.

The only way a plant will grow is if it's in good soil not dirt.

He is our soil!

Yeshua is the Root, Holy Spirit is the Water, Abba sends the increase.

Spreading the good news is the truth but it's not all we are called to do.

Casting out devils and healing the sick is a part of it too, but we must establish a home for Him down here while we are living breathing proof.

As for you, when is the last time you asked Abba what to do?

How are you advancing His Kingdom?

Lately have you made any moves?

Will you answer the call when He sends for you?

Shevat 19 5781 2:33 am

Suffering

1 Peter 4:16 KJV

"Yet if any man suffer as a Christian, let him not be ashamed; but let him glorify God on this behalf."

Sufferance is my portion.

The world rejected Christ so it may reject me too.

I'm made in the image and likeness of God so persecution is my destiny.

When the world sees me, they should see Christ!

Crucifixion is part of a believer's legacy.

Walk by faith not by sight!

When you face trials of any kind, know God is never far behind.

Seated at the right hand of power is Christ, if we suffer along His side, with Him we will be glorified.

They may not accept you.

Masses didn't accept Him either.

Yeshua is the Bread of life, but the world wants pita.

Pick up your cross and walk after Him, beat your flesh into subjection.

If you can't stand the heat, get out of the kitchen.

The Blood cleanses all!

Live for Him because He died for you!

He suffered for the sins of the whole world, yet He never committed one.

We don't deserve His love, yet He gives us all more than enough.

Pray for your brothers and sisters that are dying for His Word.

Count the cost and see if the flesh is better than the price your soul is worth.

He paid for you with His Blood.

Are you willing to shed some of yours in return?

February 5th, 2021 8:16 pm

Mirror

When you look in the mirror, who do you see?

Do you look at yourself physically or spiritually?

Naturally you are made in the image of God.

Supernaturally what is your make up?

All flesh and no spirit rouses the Lord's anger.

Do you see you on the surface or do you dig deeper?

I know on Earth we say we got our brothers, but are you your brother's brother's keeper?

Let's dive deeper.

Are you watching out for your sister's sister's features?

If you're wondering; I'm talking about you!

Is it tough to look into that mirror and see who is looking back at you?

Ever read the book of James in chapter 1 starting at verse 22?

That same James that didn't look at his brother for who He was is the same way that you're viewing yourself.

There's no need for you to keep refusing yourself.

Stop confusing yourself!

ENOUGH IS ENOUGH!

Look in that mirror and understand this; to love others, first you must love yourself!

Give yourself a hug, show yourself some love!

Remember, you were made in the image and likeness of the One who sits above.

February 8th, 2021 9:30 pm

Wisdom

"Buy wisdom and sell it not."

Wise words from the wisest man that ever walked this Earth.

Wisdom was the first brought forth from the Lord.

Knowledge is the key to understanding.

Wisdom is understanding how to use the knowledge you have.

If you're seeking wisdom seek and ask Abba for more.

You can never have too much of this, I am sure.

There are two kinds here on Earth.

God's perfect and holy wisdom and wisdom that comes from below the dirt.

Relying on the ways of this Earth will get you hurt.

Ask Solomon, when much is given, much is required.

Discernment comes with learning, that follows a burning desire.

Holy Spirit unlocks the secrets to Abba's hidden mysteries.

Literally I'm not talking figuratively!

Knowledge is power; everything is spiritual, but don't forget the physical.

The beginning of wisdom is the fear of the Lord!

Obedience and brilliance go hand in hand.

We must operate and walk in faith in order to properly understand.

No amount of wisdom can fully reveal to us Your plans.

Operating in Your frequency draws us closer to You and keeps us under Your right hand.

February 11th, 2021 10:49 pm

Jealous

Jealous.

One of the many names of God.

We shall have nothing else above Him.

Nothing!

No one and nothing can even compare!

He made us.

He deserves all of His creation.

There's no debate!

He is who He is and is worthy of His name.

Worthy of all praise, let everything that has breath praise the Lord!

I don't know another that arranged the organs in the body to operate differently, but they all work together for the same goal.

He sent us Holy Spirit because there are mysteries that can never be explained.

We will get all the answers when we dwell with Him one day.

Words are just words when they have no weight, but something happens in the atmosphere when I say this phrase: Yahweh I'm Yours!

Jealous I belong to you!

You're not a man that You should lie, Your Word is tried and true.

Instead of trying to do what the flesh is trying to do, I must abide in You.

Anything placed above or before You becomes an idol.

You frown on idolatry because You have no rival!

Adar 3 5781 5:15 pm

Write

Abba says, "Write when I speak."

His words are precious, and they hold weight.

There is meaning to everything He has to say.

Don't let complacency wash it away.

He doesn't waste breath.

The same breath in Him is in you!

You listen to yourself, don't you?

If Moses never wrote we wouldn't know how things unfolded in ages past.

Get a notebook and pen down what He places in your spirit.

Impartation is pointless if you don't absorb it.

Words have significance and knowledge is power!

He has given us the ability to read.

Write what He speaks, then read, it cuts deep.

We can't remember it all, but we must write down as much as we can.

I get it, the next time He speaks you might not have a pen in your hand, but you'll probably have your phone.

When we just listen, it enters one ear and is likely to exit the other one freely.

If you write something He tells you, down the line read.

The Word of God is the ultimate foundation!

Do you listen to the words God gives You when He's speaking?

Write them down when you can, remembering isn't always easy.

Adar 4 5781 2:10 pm

Hunger Pains

Currently I write this with pain in my belly.

My spirit is yearning yet so is my flesh.

My spirit cries, "Don't give in!"

My flesh says, "It's okay to slip."

Aching is a sign of two things, weakness and strength.

For a muscle to grow, first it must be torn apart.

Where is your heart?

Is your mind strong enough?

What and who is willing you?

Are you only satisfied when the former thing that satisfied is filling you?

Food is temporary.

All things temporary will soon fade away.

The flesh cannot walk through those gates; you must put it to death today!

Is your spirit starving because your flesh is full?

Tell me, how does your belly feel?

What is sustaining you?

Bad carbs don't taste better than good ones.

Stop eating and believing what the enemy is feeding you!

Adar 6 5781 9:58 pm

FAITH

Faith is a foundational necessity!

As humans we over complicate and turn it into a complexity.

Christ is the CornerStone and the Foundation!

We must follow Holy Spirit's lead.

Faith is stamped and must be sealed in the ground we walk on, or our faith will be walked on.

Abba drive us to reach goals so high that we can only achieve them with You.

We declare purity of thought!

The Helmet of Salvation is one of our best tools!

It's not easy on this walk expect some bumps and prepare to get bruised.

Can't lie to yourself and think it's a piece of cake.

Don't get out of bed without picking up your Shield of Faith!

Beware knowledge puffs up like soufflé, rest comfortability in the knowledge of the Way!

Don't hold fast to what you see.

Abba says, "Have faith in Me."

It's impossible to walk in faith while walking with fear.

Have faith, you're never alone!

The Heavenly Father is always near!

Adar 7 5781 3:43 pm

Fruit

What kind of fruit does your tree bear?

Can you get it anywhere or is it rare?

Does it contain goodness, kindness, and peace?

Is the branch that bears it alive or has the act of photosynthesis ceased?

Is there any love?

Is there someone around that you can help?

Are you treating your neighbor as you treat yourself?

Have you been watered lately or is your source of water on a shelf?

Is your fruit sweet or bitter to the taste?

When fear attempts to kill the root, do you have the faith to put it in its place?

Is purity of nature occupying the source of your tree's base?

What are you rooted in?

Who are you connected to?

Are you abiding in rich soil or are you on a foundation of dirt?

This world is fallen.

Are you aiding in the effort to bring life to the Earth?

Joy, long-suffering, gentleness, and self-control are pieces of the one fruit we should seek to hold!

These are all traits of the living God; we are in His image so these are characteristics we all must actively seek to uphold!

February 22nd, 2021 12:40 pm

Name

Yahweh knows you by name!

Your name is important to Him.

A name is everything, it's how you are known.

The name of Jesus is the name above all names!

Truly believing in the power of His name is how we are saved.

There is no greater name!

Demons flee and tremble at the mention of it.

Does hell get stirred up at the sound of yours?

A reputation is attached to a name.

What happens with a father is passed down to a child who shares the same.

Some are a sure ticket to a claim to fame, others clear out lanes.

Some things never change.

You can't remove a stain.

Through the Blood of Jesus, I am marked, changed, and named.

God's Child.

That's my name!

Abba's Beloved.

That's my identity!

I'm not concerned about what this world has to say.

Yahweh is my Father!

He knows me by name!

Adar 12 5781 1:20 am

Jehovah-Rophe

You are the Lord my Healer!

The Great Physician is Your title.

Better than any doctor on this Earth.

Your prescription is exactly what I need!

Refills are unlimited.

Your medicine never expires!

I can freely come to You at all times.

There's never a line and You never make me wait in a waiting room.

You always have time for me.

You supply my every need.

Bandages are not what You provide.

You wrap me with Your love and make me complete.

Fear must take a seat!

Doubt and unbelief can't compete, Jehovah You are the Chief!

You're the Best Doctor on this Earth and You live outside of it.

You are with me at all times, so technically You dwell inside of it.

When Your angels are dispatched, infirmity has to get back!

A clean bill of health is what You offer.

Spiritually and physically, healing takes place from the inside first.

Joy, Love, Peace, Gentleness, Healing, and Mercy are some of the gifts You provide.

I'll gladly move to the side; Jehovah-Rophe take over!

I need what only You can provide.

Adar 15 5781 10:52 pm

Wavering

A double-minded individual is unstable in all of their ways.

The question is do you have stability?

Does discipline and will power flow through your mind like soliloquy?

Decisions that are pivotal are not always easy to make.

It's easy to say everything is okay but in reality, your freedom is delayed.

I know it's cliché but you're breathing today.

Abba breathed breath into your lungs!

No need to waver like a wave in the sea.

Continuously flowing from left to right monotonously attempting to see what this world has to offer.

Turmoil gets you filthy.

We face it every day.

The mind is the location the enemy plays his favorite game.

Getting the believer to listen to the wrong voice is his daily routine.

If he can't get to you in one way, best believe your adversary is bringing a demonic team.

Structure is essential.

How is your mind made up?

What are your thoughts made of?

Do you have the mind of Christ or another type of DNA make up?

Trials and tribulations show what one is truly made of.

Stability or warfare begins the moment you wake up.

Adar 21 5781 11:36 pm

Food

What are you eating?

Who is feeding you?

Is the source reliable?

Does the meal come with water?

Is the water pure?

Is the spring it flows from tainted?

Is the meal fulfilling?

Does it sustain you?

Do you feel satisfied when you are done?

Is there enough for seconds or did you eat it all at once?

Are you able to digest?

Is it hard to chew?

Is it a source of protein?

Do you gain nutrients from your food?

Is it junk or is it healthy for you?

Would you share what you're eating with someone else?

Is it seasoned or lacking flavor?

Is that meal made by the flesh?
Is it prepared by God?
Does it taste like the Savior?

Adar 22 5781 11:05 am

Shoes

The foundation.

Draped over feet.

Without shoes an outfit is incomplete.

Do your shoes match your garments?

Are you rocking them because they're appealing to the eye?

Do they fit?

Are they your size?

Are you walking in something new?

Your shoes represent who you are.

Are they clean?

Are your shoes filthy?

When God tells you to walk are you willing to?

Is the gospel of peace constantly comfortably on your feet?

Are you rocking your devil stomping 3's or your sinner 6's?

Preparation comes with collaboration.

Walk with God not away from Him!

Creases come but Holy Spirit brings the reparation.
He leads us in the process of sanctification.
He is walking with us as we walk out our salvation.

Adar 29 5781 11:58 pm

Today

Change is here!

You are no longer walking in what you were walking in yesterday.

Can't stay on the ground floor like you did yesterday.

It's time to elevate!

Second place is not the place for you.

You already know what you are called to do.

You know who you are called to be.

Today is your flesh's funeral!

You get to write the eulogy.

See what you need to focus on to set up your tomorrow.

Never look back on what could've been!

Focus on what you need to focus on until the task is complete.

Yahweh says, "Behold I will do a new thing", personally I can't wait to see what He has in store!

The secrets of what He holds for you are behind that door.

Gird up your loins and kick it down!

Tomorrow starts today!

Today starts when you pick up your crown!

1 Peter 2:9-10 KJV

*But you are a chosen race,
a royal priesthood, a holy nation,
a people for God's own possession,
so that you may declare the
goodness of Him who has called you
out of darkness into His
marvelous light. In times past, you
were not a people, but now you are
the people of God. You had not
received mercy, but now you have
received mercy.*

You made it to the end!
How was the book?
Did you read it at your desk?
Or in your reading nook?
Wherever you read this,
it blesses me that you did.
Follow my journey on YouTube &
Instagram so you can hear more of this.

YouTube
Noiz_SKR

Instagram
noizskr

Made in the USA
Middletown, DE
13 May 2023

30219298R00066